CW01432902

# Contents

# Introduction

The last of the air-cooled models, the Porsche 993 evolved into the water cooled Porsche 996 in 1997 and the new Porsche 997 series first appeared in July 2004.

Initially only the Porsche 997 Carrera and the Porsche 997 Carrera S were available. The Porsche 997 Carrera had a 3.6 litre engine producing 325hp while the Porsche 997 Carrera S had a 3.8 litre engine producing 355hp. Both cars were available in Coupé and Cabriolet form. The rear wheel drive Porsche 997 Carrera and 997 Carrera S were 38 millimetres (1.5 inches) wider than the Porsche 996 C2 they replaced and they therefore had a more aggressive look. The Porsche 997 was very aerodynamic and had a Cd of 0.28.

Twelve months after the Porsche 997 Carrera and Carrera S appeared came the Porsche 997 Carrera 4 and 4S in both Coupé and Cabriolet form. These cars were 44 millimetres (1.73 inches) wider over the rear wheel arches than the standard Porsche 997 Carrera.

The Porsche 997 Carrera S Cabriolet seen here in High Street Kensington. 4058 Porsche 997 Carrera S Cabriolets were produced in 2005, 5714 in 2006 and 3141 in 2007.

The Porsche Carrera S seen here in South Kensington. The 997 Carrera S has 19 x 8J front wheels with 235/35ZR 19 tyres and 19 x 11J rear wheels with 295/30ZR 19 tyres.

**The 997 Carrera S Cabriolet featured bi-xenon headlights.**

| Gearbox | |
|---|---|
| Type | 6-speed manual |
| Ratio's | Mph per 1000 rpm |
| 1st | 3.91 / 5.7 |
| 2nd | 2.32 / 9.7 |
| 3rd | 1.66 / 13.5 |
| 4th | 1.28 / 17.5 |
| 5th | 1.08 / 20.8 |
| 6th | 0.88 / 25.5 |
| Final Drive | 3.44 |

| Porsche 997 Carrera S 7 Speed (PDK) Gearbox | |
|---|---|
| **Gear Ratios** | |
| 1st | 3.91 |
| 2nd | 2.29 |
| 3rd | 1.65 |
| 4th | 1.30 |
| 5th | 1.08 |
| 6th | 0.88 |
| 7th | 0.62 |
| Final Drive Ratio | 3.44 |
| | |

Vehicle Identification Numbers for the 997 Cabriolet S ran from 995S7 60061 to 995S7 65000 for model year 2005.

Vehicle Identification Numbers for the 997 Coupe S ran from 995S7 30061 to 995 S7 40000 for model year 2005.

For model year 2005, 997 Coupe S and 997 Cabriolet S Engine Numbers ran from 685 00501 to 685 60000.

The Porsche 997 Carrera had Engine Type M96/05 and in 2005 production was 6239 cars.

| Year | Vehicle Type | Vehicle Identification Numbers | Engine Type |
|---|---|---|---|
| 2005 | 997 Coupe | 995S7 00061 to 995S7 10000 | M96.05 |
| 2005 | 997 Coupe (USA, CDN, MEX, BR) | 995S7 15061 to 995S7 30000 | M96.05 |
| 2006 | 997 Coupe | 996S7 00061 to 996S7 10000 | M96.05 |
| 2006 | 997 Coupe (USA, CDN, MEX, BR) | 996S7 15061 to 996S7 30000 | M96.05 |
| 2007 | 997 Coupe | 997S7 00061 to 997S7 10000 | M96.05 |
| 2007 | 997 Coupe (USA, CDN, MEX, BR) | 997S7 10061 to 997S7 20000 | M96.05 |
| 2008 | 997 Coupe (USA, CDN, MEX, BR) | 997S7 00061 to 997S7 20000 | M96.05 |
| 2008 | 997 Coupe | 997S7 00061 to 997S7 10000 | M96.05 |
| 2009 | 997 Coupe | 997S7 00061 to 997S7 6000 | MAI.02 |
| 2009 | 997 Coupe (USA, CDN, MEX, BR) | 997S7 06061 to 997S7 10000 | MAI.02 |
| 2010 | 997 Coupe | 99AS7 00061 to 99AS7 6000 | MAI.02 |
| 2010 | 997 Coupe (KOR, CN, MEX, BR) | 99AS70 6061 to 99AS7 10000 | MAI.02 |
| 2010 | 997 Coupe (USA, CDN) | A9AS70 6061 to A9AS7 10000 | MAI.02 |

The 997 Carrera S was exclusively fitted with 19 inch wheels and tyres from the start of production. The 997 Carrera had 18 inch wheels and tyres as standard.

The 997 Carrera 4S had wider rear arches, being 44mm wider than the standard version.

The 997 Carrera 4S also had aluminium-coloured instruments and 19 inch alloys as standard and it has red brake calipers and twin dual exhaust tailpipes.

The Porsche 997 Carrera 4S Cabriolet seen here with the hard top fitted.

Below can be seen the Porsche 997 Carrera 4S Cabriolet's interior.

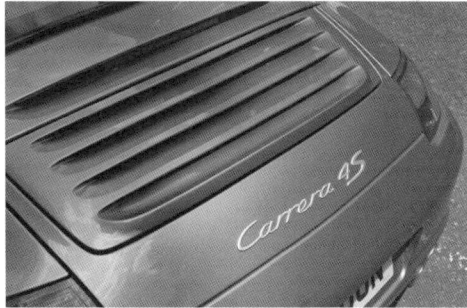

The 997 Carrera 4S has 19 x 8J front wheels with 235/35ZR19 tyres and 19 x 11J rear wheels with 305/30ZR19 tyres.

Porsche 997 Carrera 4S Cabriolet is pictured in Mayfair, London. There were 12587 Generation I Carrera 4S Cabriolets produced and 7775 Generation II Carrera 4S Cabriolets produced.

A close up of the instrumentation of the Porsche 997 Carrera 4S Cabriolet.

In 2006, 5059 Porsche 997 Carrera 4S Cabriolets were produced and in 2007 another 4372 Porsche 997 Carrera 4S Cabriolets were manufactured.

**Another Porsche 997 Carrera 4S Cabriolet seen here in High Street Kensington.**

|  | 997 Carrera 4S Generation 1 | 997 Carrera 4S Generation 2 |
|---|---|---|
| Year | 2005 to 2008 | 2008 to 2012 |
| Capacity | 3284 cc | 3800 cc |
| Compression Ratio | 11.8 to 1 | 12.5 to 1 |
| Maximum Power | 355bhp @ 6600 rpm | 385 bhp @ 6500 rpm |
| Maximum Torque | 400Nm @ 4600 rpm | 420 Nm @ 4400 rpm |
| Length | 4427 mm | 4435 mm |
| Width | 1852 mm | 1852 mm |
| Weight | 1550 Kg | 1555 Kg |
| 0 - 62 mph | 4.8 seconds | 4.7 seconds |
| Top Speed | 179 mph | 185 mph |

Porsche 997 Carrera 4S is seen here in Sloane Square.

Badging on the boot confirms this is a 997 Carrera 4S.

In 2006 Porsche made 6057 Porsche 997 Carrera 4S Coupes, and in 2007 a further 5084 Porsche 997 Carrera 4S Coupes were manufactured.

The Porsche 997 Carrera 4S seen in Dove Mews.

At the end of June 2008 details of the 997 Carrera 4 and 997 Carrera 4S were published.

Red brake calipers on the 997 Carrera 4S.

# Porsche 997 Turbo

The 997 generation Porsche 997 Turbo had a considerably modified twin turbo engine and an improved all-wheel drive system. Major modifications were made to the Vario Cam Plus System. The inlet timing adjustment of the camshafts was affected by a rotary vane adjuster. This adjuster allowed the camshaft to vary by up to thirty degrees, with respect to the position of the crankshaft.

Camshafts and tappets were configured so that the valve stroke was reduced from 11 millimetres to 3.6 millimetres at low engine revs and loads.

The Porsche 997 Turbo's increase in power output of 44 KW from an unchanged 3.6 litre displacement was attributable to new turbochargers with variable turbine geometry (VTG) that had been developed with BorgWarner. The VTG system avoided the problem of 'Turbo-lag' where large turbos were slow to respond when the accelerator was pressed.

**997 Turbo with three large air intakes at the front.
This is to cool the engine's radiators.**

## 997 Turbo Cabriolet

The new 997 Turbo Cabriolet was designed in the styling studio in Weissach. It shared the following with the 997 Turbo Coupe:

- The M97/70 twin-turbo engine with variable turbine geometry. Output of 353 KW (480hp).

- The G97/50 six-speed manual transmission with limited-slip differential, or A97/50 5-speed automatic transmission.

- The complete suspension all wheel drive, wheels, tyres and brake system.

Particular attention was paid to the torsional stiffness of the body when developing the Cabriolet. The 997 Turbo Cabriolet featured a bonnet and doors that were made from aluminium so that overall the Turbo Cabriolet weighed only 70Kg more than the Turbo Coupe.

The Porsche 997 Turbo Cabriolet had a drag coefficient of just 0.31. The split rear wing moved automatically upwards by 65 millimetres to increase downforce over the rear axle and improving stability at speed.

| Year | Vehicle Type | Vehicle Identification Numbers | Engine Type |
|---|---|---|---|
| 2007 | 997 Turbo | 997S780061 to 997S783000 | M97.70 |
| 2007 | 997 Turbo (USA, CDN, MEX, BR) | 997S783061 to 997S790000 | M97.70 |
| 2008 | 997 Turbo RDW-1 | 998S780061 to 998S783000 | M97.70 |
| 2008 | 997 Turbo RDW-2 | 998S709061 to 998S710000 | M97.70 |
| 2008 | 997 Turbo (USA, CDN, MEX, BR) | 998S783061 to 998S786000 | M97.70 |
| 2008 | 997 Turbo Cabriolet RDW-1 | 998S786061 to 998S788000 | M97.70 |
| 2008 | 997 Turbo Cabriolet RDW-2 | 998S706061 to 998S707000 | M97.70 |
| 2008 | 997 Turbo Cabrio-1 (USA, CDN, MEX, BR) | 998S783061 to 998S790000 | M97.70 |
| 2008 | 997 Turbo Cabrio-2 (USA, CDN, MEX, BR) | 998S708061 to 998S709000 | M97.70 |
| 2008 | 997 Turbo GT2 | 998S794061 to 998S796000 | M97.70S |
| 2008 | 997 Turbo GT2 (USA, CDN, MEX, BR) | 998S796061 to 998S798000 | M97.70S |

| Year | Vehicle Type | Vehicle Identification Numbers | Engine Type |
|------|--------------|-------------------------------|-------------|
| 2009 | 997 Turbo RDW | 999S760061 to 999S766000 | M97.70 |
| 2009 | 997 Turbo (USA, CDN, MEX, BR) | 997S766061 to 999S770000 | M97.70 |
| 2009 | 997 Turbo Cabrio RDW (USA, CDN, MEX, BR) | 997S773061 to 999S775000 | M97.70 |
| 2009 | 997 Turbo Cabrio | 998S709061 to 998S710000 | M97.70 |
| 2009 | 997 Turbo GT2 | 999S776061 to 999S777000 | M97.70S |
| 2009 | 997 Turbo GT2 (USA, CDN, MEX, BR) | 999S778061 to 999S779000 | M97.70S |
| 2010 | 997 Turbo | 99AS760061 to 99AS766000 | MAI.70 |
| 2010 | 997 Turbo (CN, MEX, BR, KOR) | 99AS766061 to 99AS770000 | MAI.70 |
| 2010 | 997 Turbo (USA, CDN) | A9AS766061 to A9AS770000 | MAI.70 |
| 2010 | 997 Turbo Cabrio RDW | 99AS770061 to 99AS773000 | MAI.70 |
| 2010 | 997 Turbo Cabrio (CN, MEX, BR, KOR) | 99AS773061 to 99AS775000 | MAI.70 |
| 2010 | 997 Turbo Cabrio (USA, CDN) | A9AS773061 to A9AS775000 | MAI.70 |

The Porsche 997 Turbo S seen here in a Sloane Square Mews.

Porsche claims the 997 Turbo to be the first road car with an actively controlled four-wheel-drive system.

| Porsche 997 Turbo Acceleration in Gears | | | | | |
|---|---|---|---|---|---|
| MPH | 2nd | 3rd | 4th | 5th | 6th |
| 20 - 40 | 1.9 | 3.4 | 4.6 | - | - |
| 30 - 50 | 1.5 | 2.4 | 3.5 | 4.9 | - |
| 40 - 60 | 1.5 | 2.0 | 2.7 | 3.7 | 7.3 |
| 50 - 70 | 1.6 | 2.1 | 2.4 | 3.1 | 4.6 |
| 60 - 80 | - | 2.1 | 2.6 | 3.2 | 3.8 |
| 70 - 90 | - | 2.2 | 2.7 | 3.3 | 3.8 |
| 80 - 100 | - | - | 2.8 | 3.4 | 3.8 |
| 90 - 110 | - | - | 3.9 | 3.5 | 4.0 |
| 100 - 120 | - | - | 3.0 | 3.7 | 4.3 |
| 110 - 130 | - | - | - | 4.0 | 4.8 |
| 120 - 140 | - | - | - | 4.3 | 5.4 |
| 130 - 150 | - | - | - | 4.5 | 6.1 |

| Engine | |
|---|---|
| Engine Type: | M97/70 |
| Displacement: | 3600 cc |
| Bore & Stroke: | 100mm x 76.4mm |
| Compression Ratio: | 9.01 to 1 |
| Specific Output: | 131bhp per litre |
| Power/Torque to weight: | 298 bhp/288lb ft per tonne |
| Maximum Engine Speed: | 6750rpm |
| 0 - 62 mph (Manual): | 4.6 seconds |
| 0 - 62 mph (automatic): | 5.1 seconds |

**The PTM system on the 997 Turbo introduces active front axle drive via an electronically-controlled, electromagnetically-operated multiple clutch.**

| Transmission | | |
|---|---|---|
| Gearbox: | 6-speed manual | |
| | Ratios | mph per 100 rpm |
| 1st | 3.82 | 6.1 |
| 2nd | 2.14 | 10.9 |
| 3rd | 1.48 | 15.8 |
| 4th | 1.18 | 19.8 |
| 5th | 0.97 | 24.1 |
| 6th | 0.79 | 29.6 |
| Final Drive Ratio | 3.33 | |

**The Porsche 997 Turbo weighs less than its predecessor the Porsche 996 Turbo.**

**Maximum Speed in Gear**

| 50 mph | 116 mph | 180 mph |
|--------|---------|---------|
| 8400 rpm | 8400 rpm | 8400 rpm |

( 1 )          ( 3 )          ( 5 )

( 2 )          ( 4 )          ( 6 )

| 84 mph | 148 mph | 192 mph |
|--------|---------|---------|
| 8400 rpm | 8400 rpm | 7790 rpm |

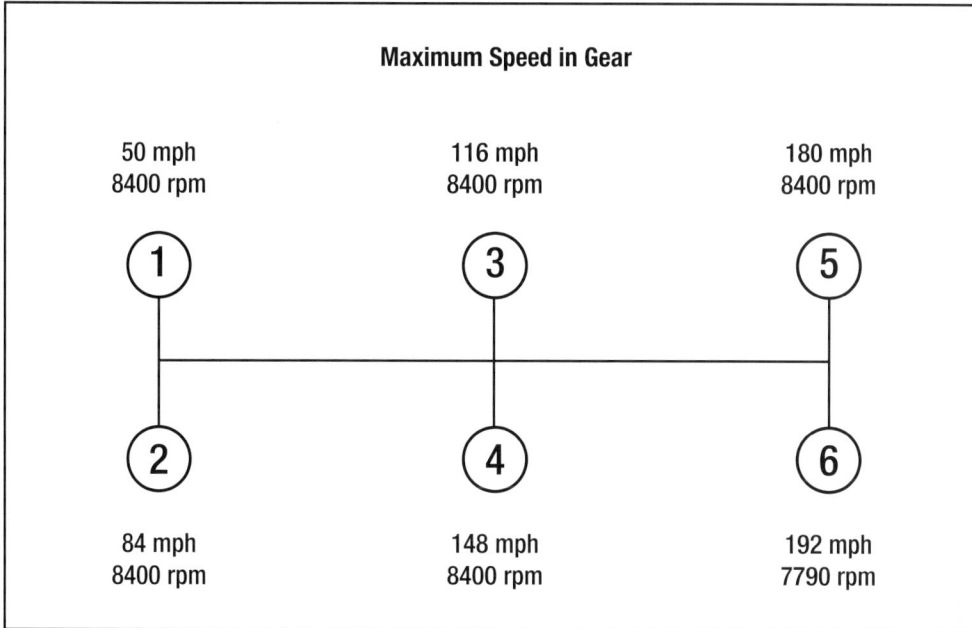

The Porsche 997 Turbo weighs 1585kg. From August 2009, 997 Turbo's were Generation 2 models with a 3.8 litre engine, and an all new PDK double-clutch 7-speed transmission. There were also **LED** front and rear lights and titanium vents.

The Porsche 997 Turbo Coupe had PCCB carbon-fibre-reinforced ceramic brakes available as an optional extra.

As well as releasing the Generation 2 Porsche 997 Turbo in May 2010, Porsche also launched the Porsche 997 Turbo S. It was a regular Porsche 997 Turbo with every desirable option included as standard.

The Porsche 997 Turbo S also delivered a maximum power of 530hp (388 KW) and this was maintained consistently from 6250rpm to 6750 rpm. On the Porsche 997 Turbo S maximum torque had also been increased and was now 700 Nm/516 ft.

This was available from 2100 rpm to 4250 rpm on the 997 Turbo S.

Compared to the Porsche 997 Turbo the 997 Turbo S had the Sports Chrono Pack Plus Porsche Ceramic Composite Brakes, Porsche Torque Vectoring, Lightweight 19inch RS Spyder alloy wheels, PDK double clutch transmission, two-tone leather, modified front wheel mounts and a carbon fibre air-intake box with a Turbo S logo. Adaptive Sports Seats with memory and cruise control were also standard on the Porsche 997 Turbo S.

**Turbo S can be seen in the instrument cluster**

**Centre-lock wheels with the extremely powerful ceramic braking system.**

**Turbo S logo on sides of the car**

| Porsche 997 Turbo and Turbo S Production Numbers | |
|---|---|
| **Generation I Cars** | |
| 997 Turbo Coupe | 15526 |
| 997 Turbo Cabriolet | 6099 |
| | |
| **Generation II Cars** | |
| 997 Turbo Coupe | 3301 |
| 997 Turbo Cabriolet | 1752 |
| 997 Turbo S Coupe | 3095 |
| 997 Turbo S Cabriolet | 2055 |
| 997 Turbo Coupe 918 Spyder | 38 |
| 997 Turbo Cabriolet 918 Spyder | 37 |
| 997 Turbo S Coupe 918 Spyder | 41 |
| 997 Turbo S Cabriolet 918 Spyder | 30 |

**The Porsche 997 Turbo S seen here in South Kensington, London.**

The Porsche 997 Turbo S achieves 0 - 62mph in 3.3 seconds. The corresponding figure for its predecessor, the 996 Turbo S was 4.2 seconds.

| 997 Turbo S Generation 2 PDK Gear Ratios | |
|---|---|
| 1st | 3.91 |
| 2nd | 2.29 |
| 3rd | 1.58 |
| 4th | 1.18 |
| 5th | 0.94 |
| 6th | 0.79 |
| 7th | 0.62 |
| Reverse | 3.55 |
| Final Drive | 3.44 |

In the development of the Cabriolet the frame around the windscreen (A-pillar) was re-inforced with high strength steel pipes.

Two further roll-over bars were installed in the partition between the rear seats and the engine compartment. Six airbags provided additional protection for the passengers and driver.

Porsche 997 Turbo S has a top speed of 196mph compared to a corresponding 187 mph for the 996 Turbo S that preceded it.

Boot spoiler on the 997 Turbo S.

Carbon fibre air-intake box on the 997 Turbo S.

**Another Porsche 997 Turbo seen in South Kensington.**

| Porsche 997 Turbo Engine Numbers | |
|---|---|
| 2007 | 62700501 to 62718000 |
| 2008 | 62800501 to 62818000 |
| 2009 | 62900501 to 62918000 |
| 2010 | A-A00501 to A-A99999 |
| 2011 | A-A00501 to A-A60000 |

RUF 997 seen in Knightsbridge has registration X1 RUF, whilst below the Porsche 997 seen in Sloane Square and its engine compartment.

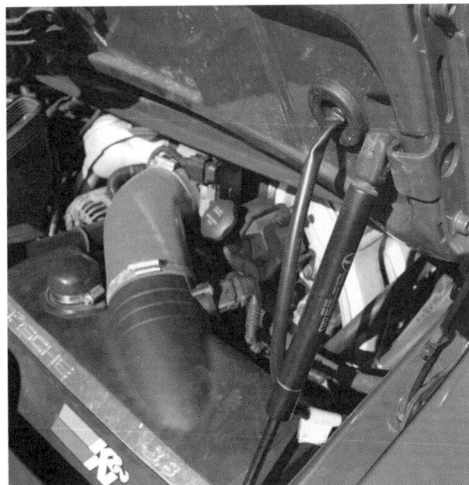

In 2007 two new Targa 4 models were introduced. The 997 Targa 4 used the 3.6 litre M96/05 engine with 325bhp. The 997 Targa 4S had the 3824cc M97/01 engine with 355hp.

| Year | Vehicle Type | Vehicle Identification Numbers | Engine Type |
|---|---|---|---|
| 2007 | 997 Targa | 997S740061 to 997S745000 | M96.05 |
| 2007 | 997 Targa (USA CDN MEX BR) | 997S745061 to 997S755000 | M96.05 |
| 2007 | 997 Targa S | 997S750061 to 997S755000 | M97.01 |
| 2007 | 997 Targa S (USA CDN MEX BR) | 997S755061 to 997S760000 | M97.01 |
| 2008 | 997 Targa | 997S740061 to 997S745000 | M96.05 |
| 2008 | 997 Targa (USA CDN MEX BR) | 997S745061 to 997S755000 | M96.05 |
| 2008 | 997 Targa S | 997S750061 to 997S755000 | M97.01 |
| 2008 | 997 Targa S (USA CDN MEX BR) | 997S755061 to 997S760000 | M97.01 |
| 2009 | 997 Targa | 997S725061 to 997S728000 | MA1.02 |
| 2009 | 997 Targa (USA CDN MEX BR) | 997S728061 to 997S730000 | MA1.02 |
| 2009 | 997 Targa S | 997S730061 to 997S733000 | MA1.01 |
| 2009 | 997 Targa S (USA CDN MEX BR) | 997S733061 to 997S735000 | MA1.01 |

| Year | Vehicle Type | Vehicle Identification Numbers | Engine Type |
|------|--------------|-------------------------------|-------------|
| 2010 | 997 Targa | 99AS725061 to 99AS728000 | MA1.02 |
| 2010 | 997 Targa (KOR CN MEX BR) | 99AS728061 to 99AS730000 | MA1.02 |
| 2010 | 997 Targa (USA CDN) | A9AS728061 to A9AS730000 | MA1.02 |
| 2010 | 997 Targa S | 99AS730061 to 99AS733000 | MA1.02 |
| 2010 | 997 Targa (KOR CN MEX BR) | 99AS733061 to 99AS735000 | MA1.02 |
| 2010 | 997 Targa S (USA CDN) | A9AS733061 to A9S735000 | MA1.02 |

**The Porsche 997 Targa 4 seen here in South Kensington.**

Porsche 997 Targa 4S seen here in Ennismore Gardens. The car has registration number "40A", whilst below the Porsche 997 Targa 4S can be seen near High Street Kensington.

The Targa roof was much improved over the previous model running the full length of the roof.

| | 2007 997 Targa 4 | 2007 997 Targa 4S |
|---|---|---|
| Engine Type: | M96/05 | M97/01 |
| Displacement: | 3596 cc | 3824 cc |
| Compression Ratio: | 11.3 to 1 | 11.8 to 1 |
| Engine Output (hp) at RPM: | 325@6800 | 355@6600 |
| Torque (Nm) at RPM: | 370@4250 | 400@4600 |
| Output per litre (KW/l) | 66.5 | 68.3 |

**The Porsche 997 Targa 4 seen here in a Sloane Square Mews.**

| 997 Targa 4 | |
|---|---|
| Engine Type: | M96/05 |
| Displacement: | 3596 cc |
| Compression Ratio: | 11.3 to 1 |
| Engine Output (hp) at RPM: | 325hp@6800rpm |
| Torque: | 370Nm@4250rpm |
| Manual Transmission: | G97/01 |
| Tiptronic Transmission: | A97/01 |

The Porsche 997 Targa 4 seen here in "The Boltons." A total of 1525 Targa 4 Generation I cars were produced.

The Porsche 997 Carrera 4 Cabriolet seen here in South Kensington. The 997 Carrera 4 was 44 mm wider at the rear than the two wheel version, and it had two oval tailpipes.

| Gear Ratios of the G97/01 Gearbox | | | |
|---|---|---|---|
| | Gear Pair (Number of teeth) | Ratio | Final Drive | Overall Ratio |
| 1st gear | 11/43 | 3.309 | 3.444 | 13.46 |
| 2nd gear | 19/44 | 2.316 | 3.444 | 7.97 |
| 3rd gear | 28/45 | 1.607 | 3.444 | 5.53 |
| 4th gear | 32/41 | 1.281 | 3.444 | 4.41 |
| 5th gear | 37/40 | 1.081 | 3.444 | 3.72 |
| 6th gear | 43/38 | 0.884 | 3.444 | 3.04 |
| Reverse | | 3.590 | 3.444 | 12.36 |

**The Porsche 997 Carrera 4S Cabriolet seen here in Mayfair.**

**997 Cabriolets models were 85Kg heavier than the 997 Coupes. The Cabriolets roof could be raised and lowered on the move in just twenty seconds.**

**Porsche 997 Carrera S Cabriolet seen here outside the Raddison Hotel.**

| Year | Vehicle Type | Vehicle Identification Numbers | Engine Type |
|------|--------------|-------------------------------|-------------|
| 2005 | 997 Cabriolet | 9955S750061 to 995S755000 | M96.05 |
| 2005 | 997 Cabriolet (USA CDN MEX BR) | 995S755061 to 995S760000 | M96.05 |
| 2005 | 997 Cabriolet S | 995S760061 to 995S765000 | M97.01 |
| 2005 | 997 Cabriolet S (USA CDN MEX BR) | 995S765061 to 995S770000 | M97.01 |
| 2006 | 997 Cabriolet | 996S750061 to 996S755000 | M96.05 |
| 2006 | 997 Cabriolet (USA CDN MEX BR) | 996S755061 to 996S760000 | M96.05 |
| 2006 | 997 Cabriolet RoW-1 | 996S760061 to 996S765000 | M97.01 |
| 2006 | 997 Cabriolet S (USA CDN MEX BR) | 996S765061 to 996S771000 | M97.01 |
| 2006 | 997 Cabriolet S RoW-1 | 996S775000 to 996S780000 | M97.01 |

| 997 Generation I Cars 6 Speed Manual Transmission Types | | |
|---|---|---|
| **Transmission Type** | **Engine Type** | **Model Application** |
| G97.01 | M96.05 | Carrera Model Range |
| G97.31 | M96.05 | Carrera 4 Model Range |
| G97.01 | M97.01 | Carrera S Model Range |
| G97.31 | M97.01 | Carrera 4S Model Range |
| G97.50 | M97.70 | Turbocharged Model Range |
| G97.88 | M97.70S | GT2 and GT2 RS |
| G97.90 | M97.76 | GT3 and GT3 RS |

| 997 Generation I Cars 5 Speed Tiptronic S (Automatic) Transmission Types | | |
|---|---|---|
| **Transmission Type** | **Engine Type** | **Model Application** |
| A97.01 | M96.05 | Carrera Model Range |
| A97.31 | M96.05 | Carrera 4 Model Range |
| A97.01 | M97.01 | Carrera S Model Range |
| A97.31 | M97.01 | Carrera 4S Model Range |
| A97.50 | M97.50 | Turbocharged Model Range |

| 997 Generation II Cars<br>6 Speed Manual Transmission Types | | |
|---|---|---|
| **Transmission Type** | **Engine Type** | **Model Application** |
| G97.05 | MA1.02 | Carrera Model Range |
| G97.35 | MA1.02 | Carrera 4 Model Range |
| G97.05 | MA1.01 | Carrera S Model Range |
| G97.35 | MA1.01 | Carrera 4S Model Range |
| G97.55 | MA1.70 | Turbocharged Model Range |
| G97.90 | M97.77R | GT3 and GT3 RS |
| G97.92 | M97.77R | GT3 RS |
| G97.92 | M97.74 | GT3 RS 4.0 Litre |

| 997 Generation II Cars<br>7 Speed PDK Transmission Types | | |
|---|---|---|
| **Transmission Type** | **Engine Type** | **Model Application** |
| CG1.00 | MA1.02 | Carrera Model Range |
| CG1.30 | MA1.02 | Carrera 4 Model Range |
| CG1.00 | MA1.01 | Carrera S Model Range |
| CG1.30 | MA1.01 | Carrera 4S Model Range |
| CG1.50 | MA1.70 | Turbocharged Model Range |

**Above the 997 Carrera S Cabriolet and below the 997 Turbo Cabriolet.**

**In 2006 just 44 Porsche 997 GT3's were produced.**

| Porsche 997 GT3 Specifications for 2008 Model | |
|---|---|
| Engine Type: | M97/76 |
| Compression Ratio: | 12.0 to 1 |
| Engine Output EC kW (hp): | 305 (415) |
| Engine Output (hp) at RPM: | 415 @ 7600 |
| Maximum Output per Litre (kW/L): | 84.7 |
| Maximum Engine Speed: | 8400 rpm |

Steering wheel and dashboard of this left hand drive GT3 can be seen here. Porsche 997 GT3 cars had a Cd of 0.29.

GT3 badge can be seen on the door sills. The 997 GT3 used stiffer spring rates than 997 Carreras. The suspension was stiff for a road car but short of the settings used on the 997 GT3 Cup Car.

These are the seats of the road-going version of the GT3. The car rides 1.2 inches lower than a standard 997 Carrera.

In 2007 there were 2333 GT3's produced.

This is the racing version of the GT3 and raced by JMH Automotive Ltd.

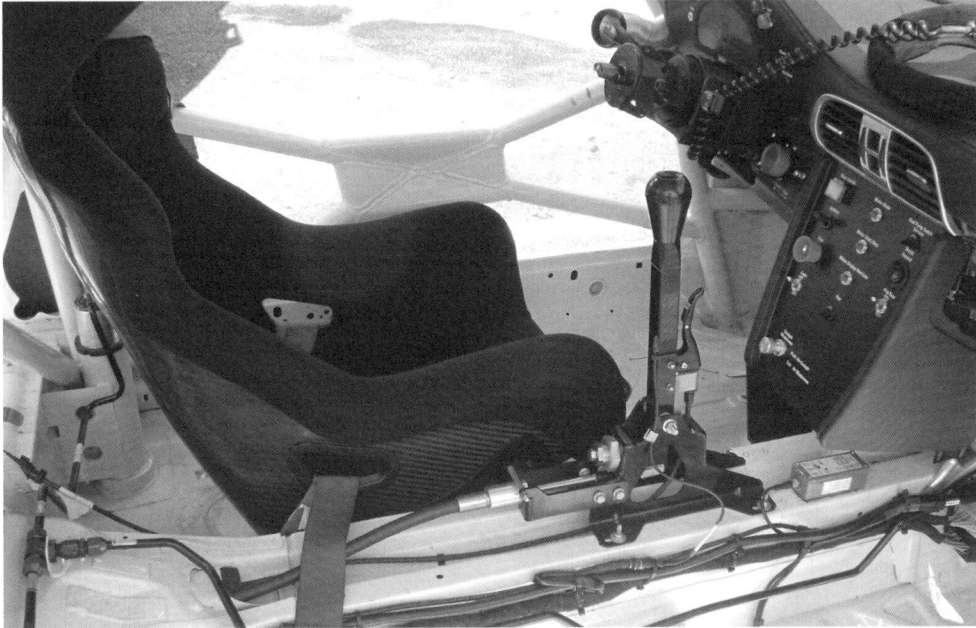

**The driving seat of the track version of the GT3 and below the cockpit.**

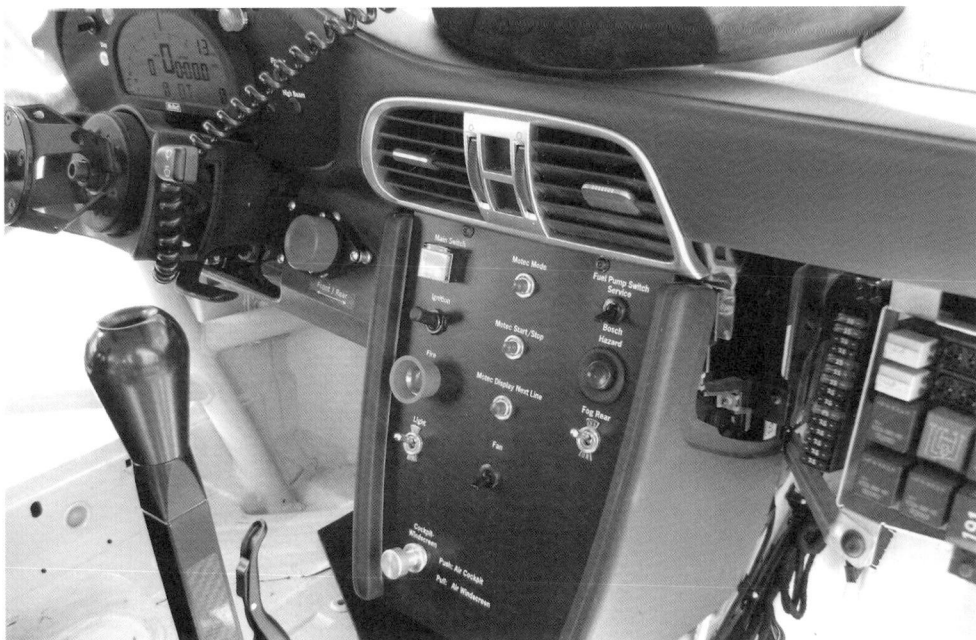

Porsche 997 GT3 Cup Car seen here at Snetterton. Doors, window frames, engine lid and adjustable rear wing were all made from carbon-fibre reinforced plastic.

To enable quick wheel changes the 997 GT3 Cup Car had a compressed air lifter installed so that all four wheels could be changed at once.

Rear spoiler of the 997 Cup Car.

Tail confirms this is the GT3 Cup Car.

The driving position in the 997 Cup Car. The bodywork was the same galvanised steel shell as the road-going 997 GT3 but with aerodynamically altered front and rear ends.

Porsche 997 GT3 Cup Cars were left hand drive.

Instrumentation inside the 997 GT3 Cup Car.

This is the engine of the Porsche 997 GT3 Cup Car as turbochargers were not allowed in GT3 racing it was the induction system that saw the most attention in order to get higher and higher power outputs.

**Above the Porsche 997 GT3 Cup Car can be seen on the track at Snetterton.**

The road version of the Porsche 997 GT3 seen here in Sloane Square.
Actively adjustable dampers were standard and Porsche Active Suspension
Management (PASM) meant an extremely high level of performance.

Inside the road going 997 GT3.

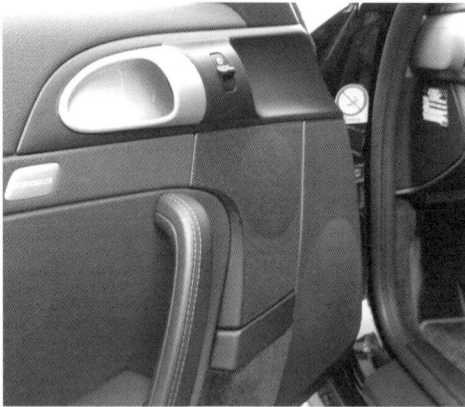

Door trim of the 997 GT3. Real leather was combined with 'leather look' elsewhere.

'GT3' just visible on the instruments in front of the driver.

| Porsche 997 GT3 Engine Numbers | | |
|---|---|---|
| Year | Engine Type | Engine Numbers |
| 2007 | M97.76 | 61723501 to 61726000 |
| 2008 | M97.76 | 61823501 to 61826000 |
| 2009 | M97.76 | 61923501 to 61926000 |
| 2010 | M97.77 | A61A23501 to A61A26000 |
| 2011 | M97.77 | 61B23501 to 61B26000 |

On Generation 2 Porsche 997 GT3's there was now the option of a front axle lift system. PASM Active Damping reacted quicker than before and the new model gained a power increase of 20hp from the preceding model's 415hp to 435hp. The bore of the 997 GT3 engine was increased from 100mm to 102.7mm taking the displacement from 3.6 litres to 3.8 litres.

| Acceleration in Gears | | | | | |
|---|---|---|---|---|---|
| MPH | 2nd | 3rd | 4th | 5th | 6th |
| 20 - 40 | 2.2 | 3.9 | 4.2 | - | - |
| 30 - 50 | 2.0 | 3.7 | 4.0 | 5.1 | 6.4 |
| 40 - 60 | 1.9 | 3.5 | 3.9 | 5.1 | 6.2 |
| 50 - 70 | 1.8 | 3.4 | 3.8 | 5.1 | 6.4 |
| 60 - 80 | 2.0 | 3.2 | 3.8 | 5.0 | 6.5 |
| 70 - 90 | - | 3.3 | 3.6 | 5.1 | 6.5 |
| 80 - 100 | - | 3.5 | 3.5 | 5.2 | 6.8 |
| 90 - 110 | - | - | 3.6 | 4.9 | 7.3 |
| 110 - 120 | - | - | 3.7 | 4.9 | 7.2 |
| 120 - 140 | - | - | 4.7 | 5.6 | - |
| 130 - 150 | - | - | - | 6.3 | - |

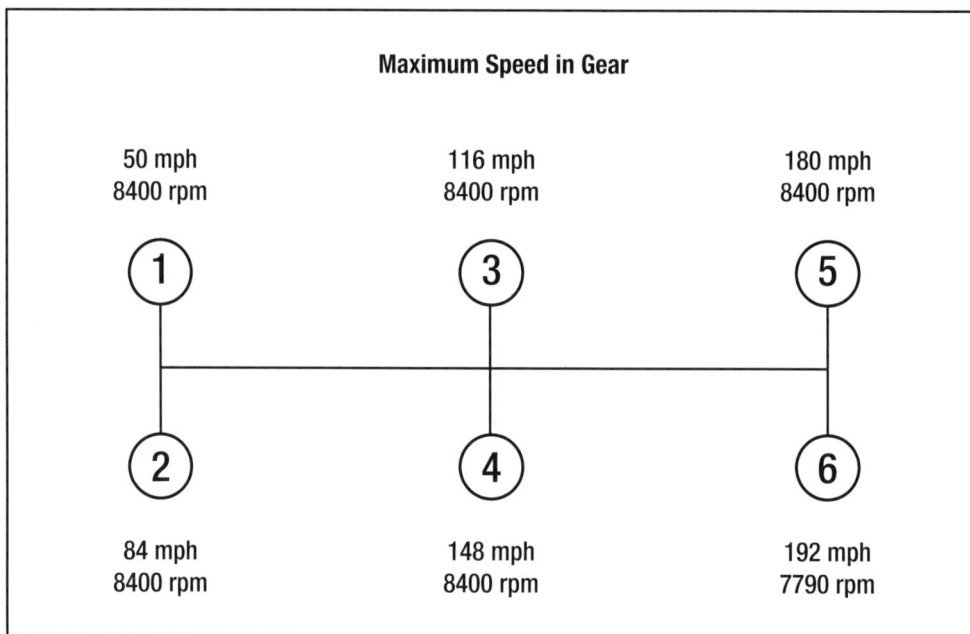

## Maximum Speed in Gear

| | | |
|---|---|---|
| 50 mph<br>8400 rpm | 116 mph<br>8400 rpm | 180 mph<br>8400 rpm |
| ① | ③ | ⑤ |
| ② | ④ | ⑥ |
| 84 mph<br>8400 rpm | 148 mph<br>8400 rpm | 192 mph<br>7790 rpm |

Below can be seen the larger rear spoiler confirming this is a Generation 2 Porsche 997 GT3.

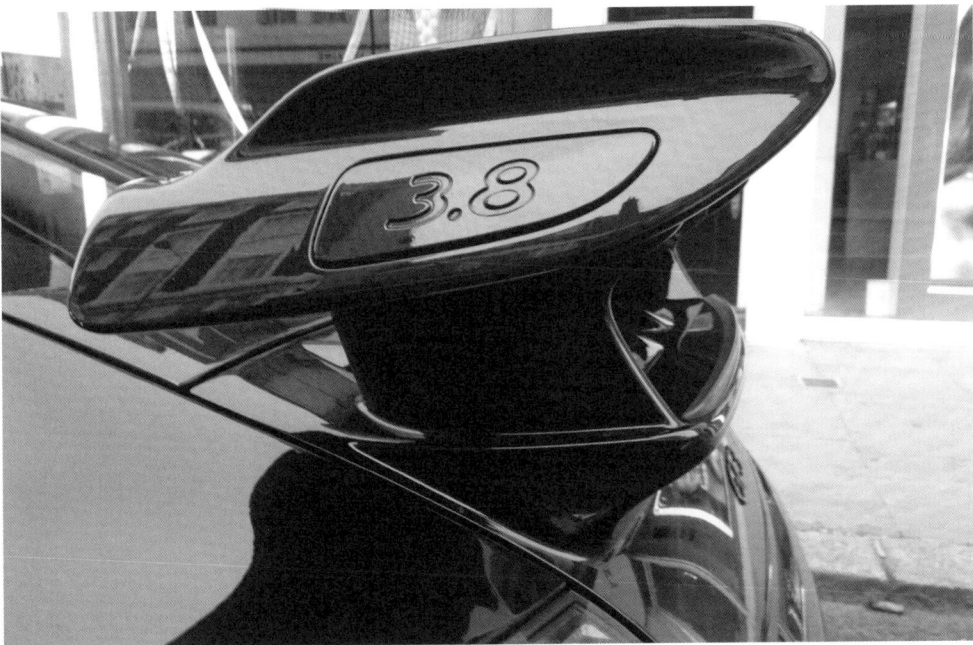

The Club Sport version of the 997 GT3 had a rollover cage, six point harness and fire extinguisher in the cabin.

| Transmission | |
|---|---|
| Gearbox: 6 - Speed Manual | |
| Ratios | mph per 1000 rpm |
| 1st | 3.82 |
| 2nd | 2.26 |
| 3rd | 1.64 |
| 4th | 1.29 |
| 5th | 1.06 |
| 6th | 0.92 |
| Final Drive | 3.44 |
| Reverse | 2.86 |

**The Porsche 997 GT3 has Engine Type M97/96.**

| 997 GT3 Generation 2 | |
| --- | --- |
| Engine Output: | 320 kW/435 hp @ 7600 rpm |
| Maximum Torque: | 430 Nm 317 lb ft @ 6250 rpm |
| Bore and Stroke: | 102.7 mm x 76.4 mm |
| Output per Litre: | 84.3 kW |
| Maximum Engine Speed: | 8500 rpm |
| Drag Coefficient: | CD=0.32 |

| Year | Vehicle Type | Vehicle Identification Numbers | Engine Type |
|------|--------------|-------------------------------|-------------|
| 2007 | 997 GT3 | 997S790061 to 997S792000 | M97.76 |
| 2007 | 997 GT3 (USA CDN MEX BR) | 997S792061 to 997S793000 | M97.76 |
| 2007 | 997 GT3 | 997S790061 to 997S792000 | M97.76 |
| 2007 | 997 GT3 (USA CDN MEX BR) | 997S792061 to 997S794000 | M97.76 |
| 2007 | 997 GT3 | 997S794001 to 997S795000 | M97.76 |
| 2008 | 997 GT3 | 998S790061 to 998S792000 | M97.76 |
| 2008 | 997 GT3 (USA CDN MEX BR) | 998S792061 to 998S794000 | M97.76 |
| 2009 | 997 GT3 | 999S790061 to 999S792000 | M97.76 |
| 2009 | 997 GT3 (USA CDN MEX BR) | 999S790061 to 999S792000 | M97.76 |
| 2010 | 997 GT3 | 99AS780061 to 99AS783000 | M97.77 |
| 2010 | 997 GT3 (MEX BR CN KOR) | 99AS783061 to 99AS785000 | M97.77 |
| 2010 | 997 GT3 (USA CDN) | A9AS783061 to A9AS785000 | M97.77 |

The Porsche 997 GT2 had a modified version of the Porsche 997 Turbo's powerful engine. It created the fastest ever road-legal Porsche 911.

Unlike the Porsche 997 Turbo the 997 GT2 was rear wheel drive only. It had 530 hp and 389 kW. The 997 GT2 had an enhanced version of the Porsche Stability Management (PSM) and this could be switched off for track work. The 997 GT2 was the first homologated road car to have a tailpipe and silencer made from titanium.

Massive 15 inch PCCB ceramic brakes were standard on the Porsche 997 GT2 and the 997 GT2 had a power to weight ratio of 368 hp (270 kW) per tonne.

The Porsche 997 GT2 could have Clubsport specification and this would include rear roll-over cage and full seat harnesses. The seats were in fire retardant fabric rather than the Alcantara of the Porsche 997 GT3. Maximum output of the Porsche 997 GT2 was 530 hp at 6500 rpm.

As well as the Porsche 997 GT2's Titanium exhaust, other weight reducing measures included the doors and front compartment lid being made in aluminium as well as the rear lid and wing being made from glass fibre-reinforced plastic.

The Porsche 997 GT2 seen here in Mayfair. The Porsche 997 GT2 weighs 1440Kg, some 145Kg less than the Porsche 997 Turbo.

**Inside the Porsche 997 GT2. The Porsche 997 GT2 had a power to weight ratio of 368hp (270Kw) per tonne.**

| Porsche 997 GT2 |
| --- |
| **Engine** |
| 6 cylinder all-aluminium |
| Water cooled boxer |
| Variocam Plus |
| Two Exhaust gas turbochargers with VTG |
| Maximum Output 390kW@6500 rpm |
| Maximum Torque 680 Nm@2200 - 4500 rpm |
| Output per litre 108.3 kW |

| Porsche 997 GT2 |
| --- |
| **Brakes** |
| Front brakes: 6 - piston aluminium monobloc. |
| Brake callipers: Inner - vented cross-drilled ceramic brake discs. |
| Diameter 380 millimetres width 34 millimetres. |
| Rear brakes: 4-piston aluminium monobloc. |
| Brake callipers: Inner-vented, cross-drilled ceramic brake discs. |
| Diameter 350 millimetres width 28 millimetres. |

| Porsche 997 GT2 |
| --- |
| **Chassis and Suspension** |
| Porsche Active Suspension Management (PASM) system with MacPherson design. |
| Spring strut axle with independent wheel suspension. |
| Cylindrical springs with active inner damper. |
| Rear axle PASM system controlled. |
| Multi - link axle. |

| Porsche 997 GT2 | |
| --- | --- |
| **Dimensions** | |
| Length: | 4469 millimetres |
| Width: | 1852 millimetres |
| Height: | 1285 millimetres |
| Front Track: | 1515 millimetres |
| Rear Track: | 1550 millimetres |
| Wheelbase: | 2350 millimetres |

**The 620 HP 997 GT2 RS that went on sale in October 2010 had a limited run of 500 cars.**

More powerful than its predecessor by 90 HP and weighing 1370Kg, the 997 GT2 RS achieved 0 - 62mph in 3.5 seconds and had a top speed of 205 mph.

The manual six-speed racing gearbox had interchangeable ratios and asymmetric limited-slip differential and ceramic brakes.

| Porsche 997 GT2 RS | |
|---|---|
| **Specifications** | |
| Engine: | 3600cc, aluminium flat-six, twin turbo, 24 valves, dohc per bank, VarioCam Plus valve operation, rear-mounted |
| Power: | 620 bhp @ 6500 rpm |
| Torque: | 516 lb ft @ 2250 - 5500 rpm |
| Transmission: | Six-speed manual, rear wheel drive |
| Top Speed: | 205 mph |

GT2 RS badging can be seen on the rear of the car.

The 997 GT2 RS differed from the 997 GT2 with matt black carbon fibre reinforced external components and wider alloy wheels and flared front wheel arches. The track was widened by 12mm at the front. The front wheel arches were widened by 26mm.

At high speeds the 997 GT2 RS has about 60% more downforce overall than the standard 997 GT2. It had a new rear wing to help achieve this.

RS versions of the Porsche 997 were built with a G97/90 six speed transmission.

The 997 GT3 was equipped with G97/90 six-speed transmission. The RS version had a non-dual-mass flywheel and bigger clutch.

Driving position of the Porsche 997 GT3 RS. Just nine Porsche 997 GT3 RS's were produced for model year 2006.

0-100 mph is achieved in 8.5 seconds and 0-124 mph in just 13.3 seconds.

This is the dashboard of the Porsche 997 GT3 RS. In 2007 there were 1095 Porsche 997 GT3 RS's produced.

The Porsche 997 GT3 RS was 20Kg lighter than the 997 GT3 thanks to its adjustable carbon-fibre rear spoiler, plastic rear lid and lightweight plastic rear window.

Not all Porsche 997 GT3's had the "GT3 RS" script along the side-skirts.

| Porsche 997 GT3 RS | |
| --- | --- |
| **Specifications** | |
| Engine: | Horizontally opposed 6 cylinder |
| Displacement: | 3600cc |
| BHP/Litre: | 115 bhp/litre |
| Maximum Power: | 409 bhp @ 7600 rpm |
| Maximum Torque: | 298 lb ft @5500 rpm |
| Power to Weight | 302 bhp/per tonne |
| Front Suspension: | MacPherson struts, coil springs, gas dampers, anti roll bar, PASM. |
| Rear Suspension: | Multi-link, coil springs, gas dampers, anti roll bar, PASM. |

# Porsche 997 Carrera GTS

The Porsche 997 Carrera GTS arrived late 2010 ahead of the launch of the forthcoming 991-series Porsche. The Porsche 997 GTS was designed to bridge the gap between the 997S and the 997 GT3. It aimed to be more comfortable than the 997 GT3 and was available as the 997 Carrera GTS Cabriolet. It had the more aggressive bodyshell of the Carrera 4 family which is 44 millimetres wider at the rear. This allowed larger 11J wheels with 305/30 ZR 19 rear tyres.

In May 2011 the Carrera 4 GTS was introduced and again was available as a coupe or cabriolet. There were 1321 Carrera 4 GTS Coupes produced and 957 Carrera 4 GTS Cabriolets produced.

The 997 Carrera GTS seen in Mayfair. There were 2656 Carrera GTS Coupes produced and 1813 Carrera GTS Cabriolets produced.

**The Porsche 997 Carrera GTS Cabriolet seen here in South Kensington.**

| Porsche 997 GTS Coupe | |
|---|---|
| **Specifications** | |
| Engine: | Six-cylinders, horizontally opposed |
| Capacity: | 3800cc |
| Maximum Power: | 408 hp @ 7300 rpm |
| Maximum Torque: | 310 lb ft @4200 - 5600 rpm |
| Transmission | six - speed manual, rear wheel drive |
| Front Suspension: | MacPherson Strut, coil springs, with Porsche Active Suspension Management (PASM). |
| Rear Suspension: | Multi-link, coil springs with Porsche Active Suspension Management (PASM). |

**Porsche 997 Carrera GTS Cabriolet has a drag coefficient of 0.31.**

There is extensive use of Alcantara in the Porsche 997 GTS.

Rear seats of the Porsche 997 GTS Cabriolet.

Note the logo on the headrest of the seats.

| | 911 Carrera Model year 2008 | 911 Carrera Model year 2009 | 911 Carrera S Model year 2008 | 911 Carrera S Model year 2009 |
|---|---|---|---|---|
| Displacement: | 3596 | 3614 | 3824 | 3800 |
| Engine Output [kW (hp] | 239 (325) | 254 (345) | 261 (355) | 283 (385) |
| at rpm: | 6800 | 6500 | 6600 | 6700 |
| Maximum Engine speed (Nm): | 370 | 390 | 400 | 420 |
| at rpm: | 4250 | 4400 | 4600 | 4700 |

| | 911 Carrera Model year 2008 | 911 Carrera Model year 2009 | 911 Carrera S Model year 2008 | 911 Carrera S Model year 2009 |
|---|---|---|---|---|
| Maximum Speed (Kmh) | | | | |
| Manual Transmission: | 285 | 289 | 293 | 302 |
| Automatic Transmission: | 280 | 289 | 285 | 302 |

| Porsche 997 Gen II 3.6 models | | |
|---|---|---|
| | **Carrera** | **Carrera 4 Targa 4** |
| **Front Wheels** | 8J x 18 RO 57 | 8J x 18 RO 57 |
| **Front Tyres** | 235/40 ZR 18 | 235/40 ZR 18 |
| **Rear Wheels** | 10.5J x 18 RO 60 | 11J x 18 R051 |
| **Rear Tyres** | 265/40 ZR 18 | 295/35 ZR 18 |

| Porsche 997 Gen II 3.8 models | | |
|---|---|---|
| | **Carrera S** | **Carrera 4S Targa 4S** |
| **Front Wheels** | 8J x 19 RO 57 | 8J x 19 RO 57 |
| **Front Tyres** | 235/35 ZR 19 | 235/35 ZR 19 |
| **Rear Wheels** | 11J x 19 RO 67 | 11J x 19 RO 51 |
| **Rear Tyres** | 295/30 ZR 19 | 305/30 ZR 19 |

| Porsche 997 | |
| --- | --- |
| **997 Generation I Production Numbers** | |
| 997 Carrera Coupe | 16521 |
| 997 Carrera S Coupe | 27237 |
| 997 Carrera Cabriolet | 9249 |
| 997 Carrera S Cabriolet | 15288 |
| 997 Carrera 4 Coupe | 3809 |
| 997 Carrera 4S Coupe | 15056 |
| 997 Carrera 4 Cabriolet | 3197 |
| 997 Carrera 4S Cabriolet | 12587 |
| 997 GT2 | 1242 |
| 997 GT3 | 3329 |
| 997 GT3 RS | 1909 |
| 997 GT3 Cup | 743 |
| 997 Targa 4 | 1525 |
| 997 Targa 4S | 3328 |

| Porsche 997 | |
|---|---|
| **997 Generation II Production Numbers** | |
| 997 Targa 4 | 1046 |
| 997 Targa 4S | 2560 |
| 997 Carrera Coupe | 7190 |
| 997 Carrera S Coupe | 9470 |
| 997 Coupe Black Edition | 1038 |
| 997 Cabriolet Black Edition | 845 |
| 997 Carrera Cabriolet | 3908 |
| 997 Carrera S Cabriolet | 6577 |
| 997 Carrera 4 Coupe | 1748 |
| 997 Carrera 4 Cabriolet | 1244 |
| 997 Carrera 4S Coupe | 9188 |
| 997 Carrera 4S Cabriolet | 7775 |
| 997 Speedster | 361 |
| 997 Sport Classic | 256 |
| 997 GT2 RS | 510 |
| 997 GT3 | 2256 |
| 997 GT3 Cup | 772 |
| 997 GT3 RS | 1619 |
| 997 GT3 RS 4.0 | 613 |